It Becomes You

Books by Dobby Gibson

Polar
Skirmish
It Becomes You

It Becomes You

POEMS

• • •

Dobby Gibson

GRAYWOLF PRESS

This publication is made possible, in part, by the voters of Minnesota through a Minnesota State Arts Board Operating Support grant, thanks to a legislative appropriation from the arts and cultural heritage fund, and through a grant from the National Endowment for the Arts. Significant support has also been provided by Target, the McKnight Foundation, Amazon.com, and other generous contributions from foundations, corporations, and individuals. To these organizations and individuals we offer our heartfelt thanks.

Special funding for this title has been provided by the Jerome Foundation.

Published by Graywolf Press
250 Third Avenue North, Suite 600
Minneapolis, Minnesota 55401

www.graywolfpress.org

Published in the United States of America

ISBN 978-1-55597-632-3

2 4 6 8 9 7 5 3 1
First Graywolf Printing, 2013

Library of Congress Control Number: 2012950635

Cover design: Kapo Ng

Contents

• • •

For Kathy
and Scarlett Moon

• • •

I believed that I wanted to be a poet,
but deep down I wanted to be a poem.

—*Jaime Gil de Biedma*

From Parts Unknown

What's undone is done.
Truancy has lost its allure.

I'm finally content to sit here
and use some of the few words

I know to mark the present
as it slides silently into the past

and assumes the mantle
of the spent moment.

There is no such thing
as breaking news,

people gather
wherever we point

our cameras.
It turns out it's the

whales who have been
watching us all along.

The First Billion Years

I once made the mistake of speaking the truth.
I chewed each bite ten times.
Before bed,
I washed my face and patted it dry.

But I awoke from every sleep sure
it had been another operation
performed unsuccessfully.
The sunrise couldn't hit its mark.
The bearded young men walked
the aisles in the used record store
without making a sound.

I didn't lose my flair—for even a moment—
to imagine myself as the person I thought I was.
There was a damn cat that followed me everywhere
and the realization that the answer
to every question I had ever been asked had been maybe.

Maybe a white wine spritzer. Maybe the movies.

I had a faint recollection
that my memory was fading,
and a peculiar habit of shaking strangers' hands,
a gesture I used
to mean both hello and good-bye.

Silly String Theory

My daughter's school roof softens,
dripping rain into the terrarium,
slowly drowning the snake.
Her ponytail, like the very filament of the universe,
won't stay bound long enough for lunch these days,
teaching me to age a little more gracefully
by teaching me to give in a little more gracefully,
just as one learns to find more pleasure
in tossing seeds on the happy couple
than in chasing bridesmaids with vodka tonics
hoping to liberate one from her catastrophe of satin.
Here's my number, a woman said to me
at a wedding many years ago,
handing over digits randomized to never connect us again,
which was like being given the combination
hidden at the heart of every galaxy,
the bingo balls of planets
being vacuumed into a black hole
like golf balls into the buggy
crisscrossing the driving range,
the one men and women older than mountains
smash each motherfucking 3-iron at.
The one piloted by a teenager
who is more or less exactly like I was at 17,
malformed and morosely mustached,
except he's four days from being worth a billion
for the website he built from ones and zeroes
to swap party pics, the one Proctor & Gamble
will use to sell us Crest White Strips.
Sorry, the more invested I become in a subject,
the harder it is for me to define the subject.
Especially when Doc is up there on the roof
hacking another skin cancer from my scalp.
He started by jabbing a syringe
full of painkiller into the crown of my head,
which was, of course, exceptionally painful,

before it filled me with powers
I never knew I could posses:
the ability to head-butt a Buick,
speculate on the supersymmetry of bosons,
or successfully receive a left hook,
which any prize fighter will tell you
requires focus on the future, like winter coming,
the mall opening thirty minutes early
so the seniors can get their walk in without wiping out.
Like us, they always circle back
to talking about what ails them
and what their kids are up to these days,
the two subjects we all know the least about,
the storefronts shackled behind steel curtains,
the scent of yesterday's cinnamon buns in the air.

After the Slap, Before the Apology

Awakening is barbarous.
Across the street, where the park casts its Moscow of shadows,
Coach takes his squad through its final walk-through,
like piano movers climbing unfamiliar stairs
to fight the same familiar force of gravity,
still slightly tourist,
still awakening to everything they slept to forget.
If you have more than you can move,
is that the definition of having
more than you deserve?
You can only hope to create the condition
you later want to describe,
disappearing into your own appointments,
into the world's unalloyed lassitude,
the tiny bike lanes as hushed and endless
as your wishful prayers for tolerance,
which arrive as unheard as a Sunday afternoon
falling through the ropes of a hammock.
If only we could get past the past,
the symptom that's become its own disease.
First we invent stuff,
then we invent stuff to make that stuff,
freeing up our time to worry about what to do next
and what kind of lifestyle to do it in,
the paint engineers creating a new hue
to give lovers another reason to argue,
the white of the moon in space,
the black of the space in space.
According to the 214 people who know,
a space walk is no walk.
It's a sweet fall and your only thought,
like you finally got
what you've been asking for all along.

What Follows Us Now Must Soon Enough Be Carried

To read the news of things both splendid
and sad happening far from me today
I had my computer keyboard whisper this coffee shop's
secret network password—*pacific*—
and it clicked it was two years
since I had seen the ocean and those I love who live near it.
Like Dean, who could see the Bay from his bed
but is now being kept alive in Texas
by a box of valves and lithium batteries
serving the functions of a human heart.
The last time I saw him our bellies were filled with oysters
and we were drunk in North Beach,
which is where I can imagine Matthew now
walks the hills with an endless twisting distorted
Neil Young guitar solo traveling between
his precision-engineered Chinese-manufactured ear buds.
I don't know whether Matthew listens to Neil Young,
but I know what it sounds like
when the fog pours around Coit Tower
in the mid afternoon as you step inside a bar
for a Sierra Nevada and a conversation about war or poetry.
Matthew has written many beautiful
and slightly tragic poems about my city,
which he lived in just long enough
to spend trapped in a cast.
I never visited him once and
in fact don't know where he lived
so I imagine it's going to be difficult for you
and probably him to believe that I miss him.
But I was a little afraid of Matthew back then,
and maybe still am, as I am often scared of people
who are larger and more amazing than I,
which feels like nearly everyone.
I can't drink beers at 3 p.m. very often
or anytime soon live in San Francisco
because I am trying to be a decent middle-class father,

which requires living close to adequate schools
and inexpensive consumer packaged goods.
Many of my new best friends
live as far from me as do my old best friends,
like Amanda, who is rehabilitating an artificial steel hip
she selected from a medical supply catalogue
while sitting on her parents' couch.
Amanda says the hip feels like an ice cream headache
in her leg.
Dean says his box of heart valves feels
like being followed by a cuckoo clock.
That's all I really know about how strange these things must feel
though I was once chased by time.
It was in Seoul, near Sinchon Station,
where the sound of a second hand followed me and my wife
as we walked with Mrs. Jeong, who had strapped
a little girl who was not yet our daughter onto her back.
She was carrying our future and my daughter's future
and my daughter's past and now complete strangers
feel the need to tell me that my daughter is "a lucky girl"
forgetting that entire shelves of memoirs
have been sarcastically titled *Lucky Girl*
to awaken us to the horrible things we say
to people who are just trying to be four years old.
According to some of these books
the presence of good fortune is something
one has to decide for oneself,
so today I thought about reaching for it
without knowing what I was exactly supposed to grab,
and I thought of that same afternoon in Seoul,
which my wife and I spent as gentle imposters
in Jogesi Temple. A woman prostrated herself next to us
hundreds of times as a priest struck a gong and chanted things
that felt as if they were about being human but also not
and a small bird flew through the temple

and kept landing on the Buddha's giant
golden shoulder. When I put my shoes back on
I knew I would spend the rest of my life wondering many new things,
including whether that bird was trapped in the temple
or had been there all along by choice.

The Barber

The only man allowed near the king with a blade begins to cut his majesty's hair. Thirty days have passed since the last appointment. The nobles have returned from Paris with their observations. The sun is out, and the light is accurate and curious.

As the royal barber works, he thinks of the weeks spent in the back room, sharpening his scissors, knowing he won't survive his first mistake. His assistants sweep curls from the palace floor and try not to think about guillotines, or even the sound of a stray pumpkin rolling down the steps.

Brows are plucked like heretics. Powders arrive. A fine mist of rose oil fills the room with its sunlight cosmos. Someone shouts, "Second mirror!" and a second mirror arrives, allowing the king to inspect the back from the perspective of his future assassin. A badger-hair brush clears his neck without confessing a whisper.

The court nods in unanimity. The silence swells, as if the entire kingdom can hear one another's thoughts, find destiny in the simplest word that tells the truest story, yet still won't save them. A little more of the day becomes a part of its larger season as the army, now without a command, dozes beneath apple trees, millet in the air. Deep in the basement the prisoners stop wailing and strain to listen, because for a moment, there's a real possibility that he might emerge kinder.

In the market, there's a great commotion as the royal coach procession arrives, the king newly resplendent. "He looks so young!" the crowd cheers. *He looks so young,* the crowd worries.

Beware of False Friends

It's autumn in the capital.
The neighbors' chickens have lost their charm.

Sometimes I think my only problem is
that I don't have anyone to talk to
who doesn't also have to listen to me.

In German, the word "gift" means poison.

How long can the one lie I tell
in every poem be
the forearm that pins the angel's neck?

I lied when I said
I would only lie once.

And I hope we can meet in person someday
so you can tell me what you think of
what little you remember of this.

It will give us something
to talk about on the way home.

This and the fact that George Washington's dentures
weren't made of wood,
they were constructed from his slaves' teeth.
No one ever saw him smile,
but from deep in the forest
his whistle could be heard for miles.

Beauty Supply

On the 21 bus this morning,
I noticed the Natural Braid & Beauty Supply
store on Lake Street
had a handmade sign in its front window
advertising *Front Lace Wigs and Fittings by Relyndis.*

I love Relyndis for daring to believe
that beauty can be supplied,
for believing in everything the used car dealers
farther down Lake have given up on,
beginning with the silver balloons and streamers
that disappeared once the economy went south.

Above the beauty supply store
there's a billboard for the Washburn-McCreary Funeral Home
advertising *Quality and Value Cremation Services,*
three white and white-haired men
in matching gold ties as shiny as the handles
of the three caskets I've lifted in my life.

There's Hymie's Records, where I found the Buck Owens LP
I'm unashamed to admit
I love listening to over and over
at least partly because it smells of an oddly comforting
mildew from a stranger's basement.

I was born on this street, about a mile from here,
and can still take it almost all the way to the house
where my parents live,
just beyond Minnehaha Creek,
my beautiful dad in his beautiful basement
listening to the TV at a volume that would scare a soldier.

On Lake Street, there's the station
where I catch the downtown train

to use these words I love so much
for purposes I occcasionally don't.

I never thought I'd live here.
The other day, when I drove Tony down Lake Street
and pointed to the hospital where I was born,
he said, "Your life is one of shocking continuity,"
and I wondered whether I was being given
a compliment or a warning.

I wonder if it was 24 degrees
on the day I was born, as it is today,
and if the light sank like it is now,
the traffic vanishing after dinner.

I wonder if, in another 40 years,
my wife and I, and my daughter, and Relyndis,
and a half million other people like us
will still flush our toilets
into the river one last time before bed

as a new set of old used cars sleeps unsold on Lake Street,
and whether there will be another version
of the man with a limp
to shuffle out after the snow falls
to gently brush them off.

Eeny Meeny Enemy

When the aliens finally do land
and decode the Greek
stitched ALL CAPS across the asses
of our sorority sisters' sweatpants,
it won't be tragic.
Whether they take pity on our polity
and teach us gentler ways,
or microwave us in galactic disappointment,
poetry will survive.
If only in the form
of poetry's mere memory of poetry,
the sound of a strange
bird's inconsolable philosophy,
the imperishable silence of a tree
growing through the windshield
of an abandoned car.
The bowl in the sink
still holds one last bite.
Raspberries ripen in the backyard,
lush with indifference.
Footsteps approach down the hall,
and as you lie in your bed
and stare at the light streaming beneath the door,
you have no idea where
you're going to sleep tonight.

Self-Reliance

At some point, which is another way
of saying now, your tireless indecision
over what to do with your life
becomes precisely what you have done with your life.
You've snorkeled in a few feet too deep. The elevator
pauses precariously before opening.
For the littlest eternity,
there's no one to meet the arriving aircraft
and unseal the cabin door.
Head north long enough
and you're eventually heading south,
but when you wander west,
you wander west forever.
God forbid any of us should get what we want.
The world seems perpetual
only to those fortunate enough
to be lost in its crowds,
and yet, the expression on your face
when you mistake yourself
to be alone is the truest you.
It's the face you make now, off duty,
the one I love the most.
This is why I sometimes feel
the need to "bother" you
for what seems like no reason.
I'm trying to set us both free—
this is my holy distraction.
Look around, my love, our little house here
is barely held together
by a few right angles
and the cumulative weight of its snow,
which we measure by the footprints
we leave while surviving it,
and the bright failure of our language
to adequately describe what it feels
like to step there, the false falling,

lightly enough to sometimes leave no trace.
In the future, they'll find a reason
to name even this day a holiday
for great events that have not yet come to pass,
so the last remaining day that isn't celebrated
will hold the greatest thrill.
Like today, for now, just the feeling
of raking a little snow
from the roof in the December dark,
which is the place I'll wait for you in the end,
our last candle in my hand.

Infinite Familiar

The crow flies in the sky.
What flies in the crow we do not know.
The woman in a black turtleneck waves her hands,
forever one sentence behind,
furiously translating the president's speech for the deaf.
The man in a Mauer jersey waves his hands,
standing in front of the publicly financed stadium's
touchless hand-towel dispenser,
thinking of the sounds his son's school makes,
windows of black garbage bags rippling in the wind.
The crow flies in the sky.
Or does the sky fly the crow?
There's that sound a cloud makes when there's a propeller inside.
There's the sound of a hedge fund manager
cursing the broken air conditioning on his yacht.
The puzzlemaster plots
two synonyms for *unexplainable*
on the axis of their only shared vowel,
the same sound you make when swinging
a tennis racquet so perfectly you wonder
whether you've struck anything at all,
sending a ball deep into the mysterious grass
where the last of the planet's sea turtles
leaves her final sandy egg.
We're in this together, friends.
But also rather alone with our smartphones, the last
of last night's Sominex still numbing our veins,
another paper clip bent back and forth
as much for the slow giving in
as for the fatal crack,
asparagus snapped over the sink,
glowstick broken phosphorescent
before the fireworks begin,
bra undone with a thumb.
In Minneapolis, there's a nightclub called Envy.
In Baghdad, there is a prison whose name means "House of Strange Fathers."

For the Pashtun children, the drone
is now their national bird.
For the wild tiger, at current rates of attrition,
the party ends in 2023.
Not as many humans are needed to create
the robots as the robots will replace,
or so says my electronic book
now glowing with LED backlighting
and fresh email, a mysterious silence
interrupting the playlist in my earbuds
like the sound of the attorney of another corporation
inventing new ways to avoid the tax code.
There's the scent of something delicious baking,
but it's coming from a stranger's house.

The Pilot

The generals summoned their finest pilot to the airbase. In a cavernous hanger whose location was as secret as its echoes were endless, they spread dozens of maps across a planning table. There were maps of the earth, the seas, even a map showing both sides of the moon.

"We want another one like this," one of the generals said, pointing to the maps, the movements of his mouth invisible beneath his mustache. "But of the clouds."

So the young pilot packed his instruments—his compass, his sextant, his drafting pencils—into his leather bag and pushed his wooden biplane toward the runway.

Once airborne, he flew over the city, looking for a place to begin. Eventually he settled on a modest cumulonimbus hovering over the bay. He named the cloud New Arkansas. After some initial measurements, he placed a pencil and a brass French curve on his graph paper and began to draw.

The winds shifted. The cloud gently changed shape. The young pilot reached for his eraser.

He tightened his grip on the plane's controls. He thought of his friends down on earth—Carl, Rhonda, Anita—and how, even though he knew their exact coordinates, he was unlikely to see any of them again.

Self-Storage

It's nothing you can give away
or even be sure was ever yours,
the mark your breath once left on the mirror,
the gasp of a Pepsi when you pop the top.
Even the feeling you get when you see
just a few horses from a great,
though mappable, distance.

In a dark corner, where you keep
your forgotten dishware and the few things
you retrieve only to help you think
about Christmas, there is an old box.
It holds a smaller, even older box,
and inside that box
something tiny rattles.

Hum

I awoke locked inside this contraption,
no room to turn around in the cockpit,
not an initial mission beyond making do.
So that when I first radioed for backup
only my own thoughts echoed in the squelch.
They became my trusted companion
as I grew old enough
to see newspapers turn into antiques,
antiques into lifestyles,
lifestyles into prisons of tasteful disrepair,
all the while the lessons of my predecessors lost on me:
do you have to clean up after making soap?
I have washed this machine in joy
and washed it in shame.
I've looked a beautiful woman in the eyes
and refused her invitation to dance.
I once built a fort out of snow
and learned that even honesty is temporary.
I have drunk too much wine and learned nothing.

At night, when the windshield darkens
and that strange state comes over me,
I drift from the present and into the great past,
back to a time before there was a man
to believe the moon was a man,
or a lone bone to comb a child's hair.
Back before there was a single secret among the trees,
or the rains washed the earth
and left it sexed,
with water everywhere and no one
yet lucky enough to suffer thirst.
Before there was a friend
to pat me gently on the shoulder
in that way that lets you know you're loved
but also being quietly asked to go.

Maybe Minorly

The ghosts are everywhere here,
in the extra place setting the waiter whisks away
and in the voices in the books you surround yourself with.
In the weird things we whisper to ourselves
about the weather and what it means,
like what to do when the lanterns freeze,
or when sailors should take warning.
We say someone is *spirited*
when they hold the ghost,
because we know we can't pass
through the snow without thinking of them
and feeling at least a hint of it,
the sound of a plow
scraping the boulevard
and then the silence that follows
and is as fleeting as forgiveness.
When the cattle lie down.
When the sparrows vanish.
In the moment the coroner is forced to decide
between *accident* and *undetermined.*
And as the worst of the storm finally arrives—
which is also the best of the storm—
night falls.
We can barely see the headlights
beautiful through the snow,
and then we can just barely see the snow.

The First American

One way to avoid thinking about
the things I'd rather avoid thinking about
is to quick list them as a means of filing them away.
Like all of the lies I've mistaken for confessions,
or the hole we've blasted in the atmospheric bubble
now larger than the Louisiana Purchase.
Or the realization that the act of
breathing is little more than the ability
to consistently recover from running out of breath.
To do it correctly, you have to forget you're doing it at all,
and if you remember, it might mean you can't,
so they hook you up to a machine
while you lie in bed and dream
of discovering electricity with a kite,
eventually your name and two dates on a stack of napkins,
another reception you'll be eternally late for.
There was a cup of coffee in your hand
where last night's champagne flute was,
now a fistful of flowers and a string with a key,
because history can only exist in the present,
which is precisely where boring old men like to read about it.
They take someone like Benjamin Franklin seriously,
but let me assure you, he really knew how to party.
When he died, his desk was stuffed with blueprints
and purple panty hose.
Like us, there were days he believed
in God and days he didn't,
but if there was one thing he knew for sure
it was that the common cold
required ridding one's veins of their demonic syrup.
What I don't know is matched
only by what I disbelieve,
and that starts with my neighbors owning guns.
I'm having trouble breathing just thinking about it.
Benjamin Franklin's dreams, well,
they were stranger than you might expect.

There were clumsy *jongleurs* struggling with excuses
and a brief pause in a storm
sudden enough to pass for The Void.
He was as ugly as your worst accident,
but he fucked his way through Paris.
He regaled royalty with stories
of Pennsylvania summers prompted
by a bite from a single strawberry and
brought entire ballrooms to tears
with nothing but a glass of water
and a mouthful of crackers.

Invidia

The future isn't the same as forever,
and to agree on this fact
is to find forgiveness.

Without breaking a sweat,
the pitcher of water finally assumes
the temperature of the room.

It is perfect.

The weary traveler
falls asleep with her shoes on,
then wakes to find them on the floor. Perfect!

You dream of seeing the great cities before the wars,
but before the wars, there were no great cities,
and to agree on this fact
is to freshen forgiveness.

In the closet, there's a jar of old pennies
almost too heavy to lift,
perfect for carrying in the dark,
perfect for your curious embrace.

At the Ready

Tomorrow watches us all day
from its atramentous parapet.
The sheer volume of our arguments
has become their only salient point,
like the memory of the morning
you awoke and discovered
they were printing the newspapers in color,
it's one more geegaw
you'll be forced to leave behind at the checkpoint
separating your life's two great stages:
answering the phone
and waiting for it to ring.

Hush now, little one, daddy's flushed his Ambien.
And now the river dreams!
The beer chases the Bloody Mary,
but what fresh ceremony will chase all of that?
In the late afternoon, the wedding shop's dressing room
littered with the white lace of near misses,
the jeweler hammering the fillings
of the dead right back into rings.

Soon the sunset will drop its false scrim
of ancient pueblo
as if there were some other, more satisfying
unit of measure than the defiant hour.
To be gullible, to be suspicious, to spy,
to defect, to go away to Florida for a while:
sometimes you have to hum the tune to try and remember the tune.

The binoculars at the overlook
may be worth the pay-per-view after all,
the scene unforgettable, if only for the feel
of the snowflakes on your lashes.

What We Have in Common Is Nothing We Possess

In my latest version of the truth,
we have to give up
to learn what we have to give up.

The bread won't toast.
The laundry still isn't dry.
The pilot lets his shoulders drop,
and the plane finally lifts.

It isn't until I turn away
that my horse approaches,
reaching her neck over the fence.

The theater has to be right
for the surrender to feel good.

We're a complete mystery to one another,
and yet my horse knows
exactly what I'm thinking,

and yours does, too.

Warble

It's not so much what you say,
but how you say it:

most babies die giants.
Blame the horrible totem

of this restaurant's stack
of empty highchairs,

an image no back
should have as burden.

There exists no map as exact as the mapped,
the river's mouth marks the river's end,

the better beckons,
the skyline, she is a false and seductive forest.

All the pinprick particles of light
we could imagine have coalesced

into the black magic of television,
and though it brings us the miracles of the world,

we wake up cold.
The sun is reducing you to shadow.

Later, the headlights will buy you
just enough time to swerve.

Pastor Pastoral

The sun sets on dinner now.
The hay bales are all stacked in the barn.
Sailboats, lashed to the buoys,
fold their arms in their laps.

No king winters here—no wonder—where
the Candle Channel entertains
those who dare remain
to slough a little skin
and build new versions of themselves,
ones composed of nothing but their own ideas and lunacy,
a few, stray wishes trapped
deep in an abandoned well.

The river goes right on occurring to itself.

There's an eternity of reruns broadcast by stars.

There are no wrong numbers here,
only strangers we're surprised to hear from,
terrified as we are of the cruel divinity of numbers,
the exactitude of our civic machinations.

Greetings, stranger, why live sorry?
We set the table, we clear the table.
In between, we call the children to supper,
and then quickly send them away.

Poem for All of My Old Best Friends

I take the ghost out for a walk
forgetting that the ghost never shuts up.

I fear the past masters as much as I fear the present,
so why do I feel like the bully?

The dream is gone once the dreaming isn't real,
when it seems exactly like it seems.

I try to write the ghost into my poem
by writing like the ghost,
but that's not it either.

Unable to write the poem I dream,
I follow the ghost home.

I whisper to the ghost.

I whisper to the ghost.

I whisper to the ghost.

—

●●●

40 Fortunes

1. There isn't an ocean for a thousand miles, but that doesn't mean this isn't beach.

2. At the necessary moment, going naked will be your most convincing disguise.

3. If you can fix a lawn mower with a pen knife, you are a funny old man.

4. Desert crossings are impressive only if the desert has been given an ominous name. Go forth and name your deserts.

5. Only fools ride the train facing backwards.

6. Among life's great injustices: no commemorative stamp has been issued in your honor, while several have been for Muppets.

7. Rare is the picnic that doesn't spread itself atop a snowman cemetery.

8. If you're alive enough to feel lighter, then the appendectomy was a success.

9. Muppets, appendectomy, snowman: the longer a list grows, the more suspicious its lacunae.

10. Years from now, you will need this combination to escape: Right: 23. Left: 14. Right: 8.

11. No matter who walks with you into the woods, you walk into the woods alone.

12. Your Nature Number is 27. Your Destiny Number is 14. Your idea of a decent stir fry is an abomination.

13. Here is the name of the person who truly loves you the most: ███████ ███████████████.

14. Life is full of little disappointments. The country of Turkey has no state bird.

15. Art is the uneraseable image: on your mother's kitchen counter, a bouquet of knives.

16. You don't realize how cruel you can be. Do you find bandanas funny simply because poor people use them as handkerchiefs?

17. Accident is as sure a path to insight as will. The inventor of the typewriter, for instance, was trying to create a prosthetic for the blind.

18. Every bridge gives the traveler two destinations, though one is always retreat.

19. Do not reveal your deceit lest you reduce it to mere crime.

20. The dream state is the only beautiful form of suffocation.

21. With friends by your side, fight with your fists. With a wall at your back, fight with compliments.

22. The ploughman prays for rain; the roof of your mouth for the pizza to cool; what are our thirties supposed to be good for again?

23. "That *was* the audition," says the avant-garde director, "and you nailed it! We're looking to cast someone who knows how to stand in line nervously."

24. Your life, like a Ferris wheel, will ultimately deliver you facing backwards at a destination that looks suspiciously similar to your initial point of departure.

25. "Daddy, I'm afraid of dying," says the little girl. "But there's nothing to be afraid of, silly," says the father, suddenly terrified of his child.

26. God is the only one among us who has mastered invisibility. This space has been intentionally left blank.

27. "Son, I am not really your father," says the old man. "Father," responds the young man, "it's too late."

28. Bald men know.

29. If that cloud looks like a lion, what does a lion look like? Answer: the statues outside the museum. People used to go there to see what a naked lady looks like.

30. We fuck what we think we lack.

31. Write your phone number here: _____. Drop this in public. Something wonderful is about to happen.

32. Show a scientist the moon and he'll tell you how it got there. Show a poet the moon and he'll start thinking about your wife.

33. Read frequently, but beware of being read to, too close it is to being told what to do.

34. Do not aspire to be the tiger. Aspire to be the sparrow who knows how to sit upon the tiger's back.

35. "No ideas but in things," reads our guidebook as we continue to refine our list: moon, sparrow, tiger's back.

36. A one-line poem called "Upon Leaving the Infertility Clinic": Six times I tried to tie my necktie, and not once did I get it right.

37. The reporter of any miracle tells a lie.

38. You don't have to travel farther than the birth canal to be born a wanderer.

39. Let the leaves forget the tune that the wind can never quite blow. Then forget the leaves.

40. Beware of the wolves. They've been raised by wolves.

Ago

Once I gave my baby a second name,
it inspired a third.

Once I drove three hundred miles just to walk
into the ocean, then turned back.

Even when I'm still hungry,
I'm known to resist the last morsel
on the shared plate,
because the truest forms of respect
are demonstrated silently.

So I have nothing against nothing.

From the backs of the books I love and am terrified by,
the great thinkers stare back at me
with little encouragement.
I am prepared to follow them anywhere!

But despite all of my studies, how could I have known
this is how my life would play out,
the bridge folding open
and stopping traffic for miles,
all for your beautiful red boat?

The Briars

Of all the words
I've fallen in and out of love with,
occupied and banished,
I haven't regretted one.

Not catacombs or marquee. Not intelligentsia.

I'm only 40 and already
I can't believe
how long a life can last.

In the empty factory,
the night watchman sits on his stool
and watches the night,
watches his watch.

His jacket, hung from the hook,
is the other version of himself,
the one still forced to stand in corners
and contemplate what he's done.

Sometimes it can get so quiet in here
that my own breath
feels like an invasion
I have to fend off,
even though holding it
provides no rescue.

Language is everything.

It's the sparrow's tracks
in the snow,
the little tyrant's fist
striking the map table.

The only expectation
is the expectation for more.

That is our silent birthright.
That is our noisy, endless war.

The Minneapolis Poem

When I see an airplane pass overhead
I sometimes imagine there are celebrated poets
reclining inside the pressurized cabin,
flying over me on their way back and forth
between New York and San Francisco
to give thrilling readings to one another
and afterward sip chablis and laugh
knowingly about books I've neither heard of nor read.
When they look down briefly at the Mississippi
they think of miserable James Wright
or miserable John Berryman,
or the strangely underwhelming poetry of Robert Bly.
Do they know the Microsoft of this little city
used to be that river, which powered the flour mills
that for some created great fortunes?
When I was young, one of the great mills exploded
after a squatter ashed his cigarette,
and a transformative civic fire raged into a cold night.
When it was over we drove past the ruins
firemen had encased in jagged sculptures of ice.
We sometimes still call this town Mill City
even though the last of the mills
have been converted into multi-million dollar lofts
for retired financial services professionals,
with stainless steel restaurant-grade appliances,
and bathroom floors lined with hidden tubes
carrying hot water to keep their toes warm when they step from the tub.
This is how it can feel looking down at the river,
or last night up at the fragments of a space station shattering
as it reached the atmosphere, through binoculars
manufactured by people in China
who are not allowed to read such news on the internet.
James Wright said Minneapolis is a horrible city
to commit suicide in because its waters are so often frozen.
I wonder whether he thought of those words
when he learned that John Berryman

had leapt from the Washington Avenue Bridge
onto the frozen ground of Bohemian Flats.
Later today my job, which is not the making of this poetry,
or the milling of flour, or the recovery of cosmic fragments
from the sea, will take me to the airport where strangers
will search my body and find nothing except this poem,
perhaps forgotten in my back pocket,
and after I tie my shoes I will share the concourse silently
with people who are passing through to other places,
and for as long as the moving sidewalk
pushes us past the cold windows
I'll delete tiny messages from my phone while moving
more quickly standing still than was once thought possible,
just enough clothes in my bag to get me home.

The Window Washer

He hates being suspended in this medieval torture diaper, but he loves navigating the world by suction cup. There's nothing like the squeak of a squeegee, or being completely disoriented by a four-alarm sunrise. It's surprisingly quiet up here, where your mortal forecasts don't apply. He's tired of people asking him whether the traffic looks like bugs—but yes, the traffic looks like bugs.

It's a controlled fall through a canyon holding a reflection of the city advertising its latest version of itself, the one full of best intentions, every angle acute, the engineering as precise and unresponsive as the firmament.

He knows your secrets, because like your conscience, he's always over your shoulder, looking at what you're looking at in the alien flicker of your desktop monitor, and the nose you're ferociously picking while doing so. But he prides himself on discretion, because discretion is the window washer's code.

The work is done once the clarity is fine enough to be imperceptible. Lately, he's been trying to narrow his practice. He wants to focus on the spots inside the spots. He wants to focus on forgiveness, and forgiveness starts with the rain.

In Case Of

In the way impatience can become a means
to avoid capitulation, even the simplest business
often assumes a funny air,
my tongue dumbly in its mouth
like a young bird trapped in an old cage.
My life growing a little longer
and more worn at the edges, and yet,
I've lived like a god.
I've swum in an infinite pool.
I've lain on my back and been raised up
to see the great cathedral ceiling
from the distance of a genius's brushstroke.
May rain once filled a dog dish
as I went back to bed,
breaking the day's appointments.

Here the worried fields lend midnight
its even darker floor.
Autumn vines grow slowly in a form of torment,
the farmhouse addresses
impossible to read from the car.
I haven't found the right word for any of this yet,
another of my life's little emergencies.

Last night, unable to name the trees by the river,
we watched them shake in the wind
and listened as their fruit surrendered,
gently drumming the earth.
The plants that had been set out by day
were brought in for the night.
The cicadas had fallen silent,
though we didn't hear, exactly, when,
or realize until much later
what we had been missing.

Poem for My Sleeping Pills

Inside the little bottle,
the miners work all night.

Outside in the heat,
the interns lock arms
and comb the desert,
searching for what's left of the space shuttle.

In every direction, there's this new
generation of heavy metal bassists melting
back into their speaker stacks,
and when the song stops at the ice rink,
there's nothing left
but the sound of tiny blades carving circles
in whatever light can be thrown
across a young girl's ponytail
by the dirty mirrors of a disco ball.

You can't change the past,
but in that past you could have changed the present,
so in the future you're going to wish
you did something different now.

The miners load the chalk into the bags
and load the bags into the rail cars
and send the rail cars down the tracks
to who knows where.

There are nights when I think
every word I've ever read was the truth,
and nights when I worry I invented everything—
everything being another word for
what little I know now.

When the miners finally speak to you,
don't look them in the eyes.

Their headlamps are blinding.

No-Motion Replay

Just wait a while and the water will run clear,
like the ordinary morning renewing
its contract without reward,
like the strange shadows shuffling
behind the curtains of the nunnery,
it's no accident if it has a cause.

There are those priestly incantations that seem
to retrace your own steps
in the way prison guards can be seduced
by the sweep of their own spotlight,
or how your money can grow immune
to whatever thoughts you have about it.
Between never and soon
you found a place you can trust,
sacrificing something, but what?

Once there were pleasures you felt
you were pointed toward:
killing time among the disorganized throngs
as the snow paratrooped into the square,
and later, the lonely
valley's blushing countenance,
empty except for the mimics.

So you made a buoyant return
to your birthplace palisades,
stretching out amid the ornamentation
to which all recognition alludes,
the water running clear,
the water shallow and clear,
your memory undependable but long enough
to send you home still growing older, still dry.

The Explorer

The explorer awoke as himself again this morning. Even as the miracle of sight was restored, the pattern had grown more suspicious.

Although the alarm clock screamed a single instruction, it was difficult to know how to respond. The explorer wondered how he would record this believably on his final report.

He booked an expedition to the kitchen where a steel coffin stood upright against the wall, humming. Preserved inside, he had been told, were the remains of food.

When he opened the coffin, he felt a cold wash over his feet like a wave from a forgotten sea. As he suffered the urge to put the remains into his mouth, he decided to camp in this outpost a little longer, where he knew he could open the smallest door and still trust the light.

Waking in Someone Else's Clothes

Now that we're under the influence
of having been under the influence,
the shadow of one blade of the ceiling fan
followed by the shadow of one blade of the ceiling fan,
we can relax and wonder whether
this is how the infinite begins,
the light rising through the window
and our hearts rising back, a cloud appearing
as if one of your own thoughts occurring to you,
proving we are mostly evaporatory after all.
We should at some point introduce ourselves,
for though this is no longer sleep,
it still feels like something to wake from,
the sun repeating yesterday's pattern on the hardwood floor
repeating yesterday's pattern on the earth,
the cold making you want to give everything away
except your unmade bed and a phone number.
Deep inside these words are all the rituals
and rites reenacted by their mere use,
and deep inside the poet is the desire
to celebrate and fuck that shit up.
It's as easy as saying *glass.*
We want to believe, above all else,
that we really know what little we know,
that the nerve endings weren't lying to us all along.
There's a cloud in the sky that won't stay put.
There's a bus flashing its lights
at the tracks though there isn't a train for miles.
There's a cold that keeps our bones museumed in our homes
in shirts that smell like someone else did yesterday.
Only later will you assess your burdens,
looking back in the opposite direction
in which you're finally moving,
thinking, now, this way:
two ruts define the snow road,
each exactly one-tire wide.

The New Craziness

They do everything differently than you do
and they're saying the exact same thing about you.
Sometimes it makes me happy to see
someone shopping in slippers,
or driving without their lights on.
Though maybe not finishing a surgery
by removing the wrong kidney
and stitching the scalpel inside.
It makes me sad to remember
the morning the crowd surrounded the woman
balancing ominously on the railing
of the Lake Street Bridge,
though that bridge was ominous
long before she stood there.
What's the tallest thing
you've ever jumped from?
For me it might be Kansas.
I'm glad I can always think about Kansas
when I need to think
about almost nothing at all.
I wonder what Kansas thinks about
when it wants to clear its head?
It probably steps outside
and feels the prairie sun
burn its face.
It bathes in the germination
of the nation's future toast,
taking a long breath and thinking its only thought,
I was here first
so all that I can see is mine.

The Archeologists

Three archeologists cracked through the final wall inside an ancient tomb. When enough stones fell away to allow them to step inside, they found only themselves there, blinking uselessly in the dark.

Wandering behind the beams of their flashlights, they soon made their only discovery: the realization that their understanding of mankind's place in the world would not, for today, be advanced.

"What amazes me now amazed me yesterday," said one softly in the echo of the empty chamber.

Only the dampness was haunting, like a promise that had become an expectation to which they were suddenly held. The room held its breath.

"If you met me all over again, I'm not entirely sure you would like me, but I would try," said another. He received no response from his colleagues. He had been daydreaming of mummies. "I always try."

The afterlife remains a rumor I disbelieve, wrote the third archeologist in her notebook. *But if I'm born again, I won't be sorry.*

Together We're Strangers

Forgetting what you've lost,
you rediscover the value in loss,

the lone squirrel in the snow,
the lone snow on the prairie,

the blizzard's shock of proximity,
like a silence you'll never

find a way to talk over.
Inside the blank pageant,

you can't imagine other lives
or even the existence of friends,

so you're finally brave enough to love.
And as the light rushes in,

obliterating its own need,
there is no ideal, no catastrophe.

Stepping out into the snow, you feel cold.
Then you become the cold.

Charity Water

I have so much to be grateful for here
in this cow town that has me fenced in
without a viable escape plan
in the middle of a country
that has gone completely bankrupt.
I love my daughter and my daughter loves
snow. In the winter, it smells exactly like
nothing. Like you haven't
smelled or tasted anything in years
and have heard only a rumor
of other senses.
Outside it feels like it used to feel
back when waiting for an airplane
didn't involve watching TV on your phone.
The fish lower their metabolisms
and sink deep into a lake
that's now a parking lot for pickups.
Before I vacuum, I pick up
my daughter's giant butterfly wings and hang
them from a doorknob by their elastics.
Once when I vacuumed up her crayon
I had to buy three different
needle-nose pliers to extract it
and restore the appliance's suction.
To survive January, some fish
become so motionless that even brushing
against the frozen surface
can nucleate ice crystals,
freezing their bodies solid in a bolt of ice lightning.
Some people stay between the air quotes
and call poems *texts*.
My daughter knows it's better to dance when you vacuum
because you have to dance while you can.
My favorite crayon has always been *dancing green*.

What did that color do to deserve the privilege
of writing my daughter's first A,
and who wouldn't choose to leave the world in a flash
if they knew they would rise?

In Lieu of Flowers

I wouldn't worry about this
exceptionally minor form of cancer
if they didn't keep finding more of it
in ever stranger places.
Like beneath my hair.

Doc told me this form
of the disease
has its genetic roots
in the cells of an ancient fruit fly,
but I'm not feeling jumpy or even particularly old,
and am actually less interested in
causes than effects.

A little flourish of flamenco.
An old memory washed
ashore, covered in kelp.
Complicated flight arrangements, the wind
reversing the river,
dragonflies mating in the air.

Today this traffic is once again
doing exactly as its told.
There's the sound of a beer bottle
being hurled from a truck,
and the one that comes
right after the end of the spin cycle,
like the sound the two Dakotas make
when they put their heads
together along that long border
and still draw an eternal blank.

The oldest of my known ancestors
is buried in one of them, I forget which,
in a small town I've never seen
that the rest of us abandoned long ago
called Faith.

The Painter

The painter had decided to quit painting forever. He was announcing this to his wife as she was busy baking in the kitchen.

"That's nice, love," she said. She was making a banana bread the painter knew he would have to refuse to taste, lest it inspire him. He knew he didn't even dare smell the bread baking—he would have to leave the house immediately.

"I have to leave the house immediately," he said to his wife.

The painter went on a long drive in the snow, following the graceful turns in a road that ran alongside the river. The snow was still falling, but he didn't think about it. The air was cool and pleasantly moist, but he didn't think about it. He turned off the radio and adhered as closely to the speed limit as he could manage.

Despite being intent on refusing sleep and its electric dreams, several hours passed and he had little choice but to return home. Inside, the bread was gone. His wife was upstairs asleep. The house was warm, and it smelled of cinnamon and butter.

The painter looked out the kitchen window at the twin tire tracks he had left in the driveway snow. And as the snow fell and filled them, and as the warmth of the house buried him in the stillness of his life's most familiar pleasures, he kept watch from the window until the last remaining marks of his day were gone.

That Was Now, This Is Then

Another day passes quickly enough
to make you feel unrecognizable,
not a master of a single melody,
no allergies to medication,
very few ideas about alternative healing
or even home, part backyard, part pet graveyard,
the rest of the time a place
to step outside and have a cigarette in the cold.

Don't let the ceremony fool you,
all religions are lonely in the end.

So maybe you send an invitation
to everyone you know and hope for the best,
knowing that chaos creates the best party,
a skeleton dancing with every nurse,
last revelers leaving at dawn
as if regaining sight.

Memory: terror.
Darkness: light.

Did you realize that once your car
reaches the speed of light,
its headlights won't work?
They will no longer be able to precede you.

Beautiful darkness. Beautiful midnight
inside beautiful eternity.
Beautiful inarticulations.
Remnant, incidental everlasting.

Heart is where the home is,
and though it may take a while
for it to sink in,

you can still drag each moment as far as you can,
and pull the car in the garage,
and watch the upside-down bikes vanish
as quickly as you flip the switch.

Scared Sacred

Real people don't wait
for the quotation marks for the dialogue to begin,
I thought about saying to my dinner guests,
already defeating my own argument.
I had dreamed I dreamed the perfect dream,
one I simply had to wake from
to discover I had failed.
They were telling me to remove my belt
at the checkpoint
and turn my pockets inside out,
and it inspired me to think of my greatest secret
and bury it where even a surgeon couldn't find it.
They were confiscating excuses.
They were citing citations, stating statutes.
They slipped a warning beneath my wipers
and told me to move along.
They told me I wasn't dying—
I hadn't even been born yet—
but their every smile seemed like mind control.
I wasn't displeased with this world.
I could still touch corduroy.
I could watch the leader
of the marathon flash past in bare feet.
I knew I could take the train
wherever I wanted to go,
stopping at distant stations
to read enormous menus
of departures, arrivals and time.

Full Body Scan

They say if you can't sleep,
you should find a way to clear your mind.
Don't think about the watermelon halved,
beached lifeboat on the counter.
Forget about the mist pulling back from the field
or whatever ocean Ohio used to be.
You're going to have to go
to the end of the line
to form the line.
There are ten thousand things to say.
These are the ten thousand things!
A refrigerated truck hauls $5,000
worth of cold air across the Mojave.
A frog team rises empty-handed
from the submerged sedan,
tiny bubbles in their veins.
The lumberjack, running nowhere,
furiously spins the log.
There's the coma of another comma,
a comet that comes and goes,
the hallway light in the prison
that's always left on.
There's the sound of the sound
of the summer leaving,
if there were a better button,
you would have pushed it by now.
They say if you can't sleep,
you should rid your house of mirrors and magnets.
Down come the watercolors from the fridge.
Down come the coupons and the family vacation.
You're left alone to count backwards from ten,
like the trophy wives of astronauts,
staring into the sun in resentment of the stars,

like that moment after the storm
when you look through the windshield,
convinced you've learned your life's great lesson
whose only reward is the power to drive all night.

The Gentle Reader Asks the Poet,
"Where Do You Get the Ideas for Your Poems?"

A dumb question, sometimes. Or
the interruption, an accusation,
an acceleration away from the least believable excuse.
They form from spills, fire drills,
the vineyards on the hills,
a tiny blowtorch flashes over the dessert
and suddenly another word feels used up.
So you try to look away,
knowing that deep inside
every poem is the envy
of a far greater poem—they all begin
with that mistake.
                    By the lake,
in an abandoned barn,
or whatever washes up in the flood,
a shattered toy, the rhymes of a bored boy,
or a play of sunlight along the riverbank,
trees' scapular shadows cast
back and forth as some potential texture
in time is realized, and real enough to be momentary.
They begin
            by immediately beginning
to end—a poem is no more meant for this world
than you, dear reader—
so in the beginning's end
is but a bird's breath, a bad bet,
and the creation and destruction of a single champagne bubble
delivers the desire to be doing something else
with your time now that
you're watching the sun
stream through the leaves, gently yellowed,
and feeling for the first time in months, maybe,
just a little cold.

For Now

The river makes its only gesture.
It has no need of the names we've given it:

What Old Men Do and Know. Hero Mudbath.
The Run-On Sentence.

But even in this simple sense
can it become more than real

by being so essential to become
its own proof.

What we think we see
is what's been right here all along.

For now the only known ghost in captivity
is captivity itself.

Nocturne

When no one else is looking,
you pour yourself one last glass of milk.
The streetlights flick on.
Now what to think about?

Your version of God, maybe, or your parents.
Your future and your ambitions for it,
which the darkness forces you to admit are comic.

Behind the soup pot,
the matches sleep in their box.
The garden hose has curled up
next to the lap pool
dozing beneath its plastic blanket.
The lone fireman charged
with waiting by the alarm
shuffles his cards and yawns.

He's not so different from you.

When the lightning strikes the pavement,
he tries not to flinch.

In what houses remain, a million voices
hush to one failed speech
like the snow falling onto the glacier
that even at midnight drops
its oldest inch into the sea.

Postscript

I had hoped to find the end
already here waiting for me,
like when I awoke this morning
and realized I had spent
another night asleep believing
everything I had been told.

That sense of trust is what I miss most of all.

Even as the sun rises,
the darkness approaches.
You are the monster of your own campfire story,
and the telling of it
has been your life's noblest deed.
You can't bear to be alone,
but this is the best evidence you have
that you're still here.

In a charming café a thousand miles away,
a couple sits across from one another
and reads the news in silence.
It's up to you to choose
what happens next—it always has been—
and it's okay to choose *not much*.
Some ice snaps in a glass.
How still the world is.

• • •

It Becomes You

Even if this is the only available means

it may not amount to much of an excuse,

the cardinals picking at berries

by the road for reasons that may

or may not have to do with hunger,

just their version of speaking out or haunting

a place by assuming a space,

precisely the kind of emissaries

charged with delivering our mostly false sense of freedom.

Advantage: earth.

The weather here is always threatening

fuller disclosure or another

more complicated version of itself,

the ash leaves revealing a few signs of discord

before we're again left

to the task of adjusting our asset allocations

while backing slowly from the wall,

hoping the portraiture hangs straight.

(Are you embarrassed? I'm a little embarrassed.)

Any fidelity to the solo

is going to have to be

in part to the one ancient gesture

it's best able to present.

In the contortions of the courtroom

of the past the tape plays back slowly,

but the narration hardly changes

as we linger near the expired geyser.

Which one of us is going to be the first

to make the lieutenant cry?

And what does that sort of proposition

think it's digesting?

You, the impossibility

of the surrounding landscape, certainly,

and the politics of it—the very question itself—

as do so many of the systems

stirring our soluble space.

The illusion of diversity conceals a lack of choice,

so you're constantly looking

for something you just forgot,

until you forget you're looking and just see.

You hold your hands over your ears

and say *la-la-la* as if you could mute an idea

and your very failure to do so might be pleasing.

Yes we can!

No you cannot have my kazoo!

Celluloid is to these phantoms as fraction is to frustration,

as it is to support them, to help them through,

for the snap is the simplest statistic

we can't ignore.

Despite what you think, I'm here for you. I'm always here for you.

We dance together and dance alone

and in between

we look at one another on the internet alone.

We master search to be better entertained by search.

We're either waging or watching.

We're adorable. Our money is adorable!

Held up to the light

and peered through like pond water,

forefatherly, zeroed, whatever can be folded

into a square and slid across a desk.

So when you think of America,

you think of _____.

We shouldn't speak of it.

The night feeds our prayers, the light our wonder,

we meet in the middle, we wander,

even our time is spent.

You never call anymore . . .

Another silence ends in conversation.

The broken radio broadcasts nothing but storms,

each listener keynoting his solitary convention of loneliness.

If you're willing to wait for me,

I may as well make you wait

for me long enough for me

to be late. Which is typical of twilight,

and like any debt, it's the most urgent currency.

You can payoff the principal but you can never

zero the feeling of indenture.

The gash becomes drizzle and never dies

as we banish the antiquated texts,

detained by mutability, the said sad.

Now that the participants

have become their own correspondents,

every forecast will call for more of the same.

More filthy money, funny money,

vested, the spaces between the

acts determining the tense.

So let the call go out for a great, quantitative easing.

And not a rabbit in the snow but just its tracks,

what little is left of a small, sudden thought,

like the realization you might enjoy jazz

more if you can imagine hearing it

in a time before it was thought to exist.

One idea is to make a primitive gesture

and stand by it, unearth its meaning later

as a vessel of a remembered world.

Another is to balance the state budget

on the back of its local school districts

and say you govern for Christ.

Had it been another way, more ordinary

or just less puzzling, we might have avoided scrutiny,

swapped a little hunger for thirst,

reflections for soft thoughts.

But now that we're bankrupt,

there are only the margins to call.

The drop-downs avail us of our shipping options

as the plug-ins imperceptibly catalogue

memories into the programming

we cherish, despite the mischief.

Don't think about it, just behave—snow

is not ice cream, Brayden!

We can only get on with it.

Be it resolved: the C-suite will enhance

one another's comp packages as the capital quivers,

Beijing hoarding t-bills and proffering a fresh advance.

Right-sized, the greeters will have to greet harder

in their theaters of SKUs.

Isn't multiple beginnings and ends one possibility?

Certainly every bridge that collapses in the afternoon

still traffics in tales of the travelers who remain,

the sunlight that falls on us like bees,

the bees that fall into meadows who knows where.

Beware of the man who promises

to show you the time of your life,

for no free man who has seen time pass

has been thankful.

So you'll have the operation. You'll recover.

Heather is amused.

Sometimes the surest way to mean a note is to fail to hit it.

In the desert of middleness, we all cast long shadows.

That's where our Winnebagos go to die,

sentries of rusting lawn chairs

facing a million sunsets

as they fade into the last color

we remember from the 20th century.

You don't like your job any more than they do,

a hundred days a year spent at 30,000 feet

staring at a polypropylene seat back

holding a dull magazine called *Sky*.

Sorry, sky, you've been trademarked.

Our maps have been mobilized.

Our scuttled acts church thought, double meaning.

Each rehearsal another fragile covenant,

or so we're told by the algorithms,

which like the tiny cities of the prairie

have been strewn like cinders, a sight

of modest warmth for those born too late for faith.

This is our prepayment. This is our failed deposit.

This is my way of telling you

that beneath these vestments,

I'm wearing nothing. This is good-bye. Content is king!

Or so goes our assault

on the meager citadel of savings.

We're going to need a certificate

to certify your daughter's certificate,

and then it's panic panic picnic.

Whose turn is it to call the sitter anyway?

Once there was a time when

we would have never thought to ask

such a question. In such sunlight,

the setting feels forever false, persistently present.

The lit candle evaporates into its sudden sight.

We can be whatever we can borrow,

but we'll finally become what we owe,

and out of this little light we make the major mind,

guarding its gallant chamber,

calmed by its concomitant strummings.

We must try to hold our head high

while publicly carrying the plastic paddle

that is the primitive system

securing this venue's potty pass.

We listen to our better selves

but try not to be beholden, open to the cure

for the adjectives that continue to fail our present.

A young man tucks a thousand postcards advertising

strippers beneath a thousand windshield wipers

idle in front of city hall.

Such things no longer have to be imagined

to become so inevitably so.

The barcodes on our blazers. The debt-to-equity ratios.

The toilets that have become our headwaters.

The sky that still naively

operates its organic cloud farm

while delivering frequencies to phone bombs.

Outside, the cardinals work together

in obscurity like little poets, like layers of law,

ignoring one another

while still being fairly haunted by one another.

They make no sign, other than the very absence of gesture

that has always been their most urgent signal.

It's a strange time in the history of the end

of the boundaries between human persons,

the text now inseparable from the commentary,

the copy of the copy

of the copy, ISBN 978-1-55597-632-3.

The photo shoot's stylist mists the burger with shellac

and, voila, another image

surgically delivers its payload of satisfaction.

While we slept, some people from California

converted a few more of our libraries

into computer labs as the air conditioner,

rattling in the window,

brainwashed us with its secret code,

the rest of us marching off to a new war

where we'll declare the old victory.

What goes into the time machine should stay in the time machine.

Dusk now descends on the miniature golf course,

and as the teenager flips the switch

on the little windmill there's the realization

that the fun will be harder to come by now.

Even during these, our precious non-billable

hours wandering the broken sidewalks

in the tiny kingdom of Governor No,

we think, "We shouldn't leave one another alone,"

but it's too late. He is our king.

From his suburban turret, he dreams of the Potomac

and all of the money there they now call speech,

admiring us as we water our asphalt gardens,

the black trash bags lining the curbs like lead balloons.

We have a name for this king, and it is The Fuck.

So we naked up, lather for a bit

and then try on a new disguise.

Maybe you take your oldest shoes out for a walk

because you want the sweet scent of escape

without the sour taste of commitment,

your pockets loaded down

with quarters for the wash,

your tongue heavy with that expression

you picked up from a friend

you haven't seen in decades,

the one about an ambulance being

the little white truck

with lousy ice cream.

Have a nice day and thank you for choosing Wells Fargo.

We're furiously inventing millions of new ways

to stay exactly the same.

In the middle of the night, the laboratory falls silent

and the variables slightly shift,

as the most recently discovered

particles of matter materialize and vanish

in artificial collisions more quickly

than you can forget your dinner host's name.

These days a worker bee lives just 40 days,

a mosquito 14. Prom on Tuesday, second divorce

by Thursday, flashbulb, pork chop, night.

Clear visibility beneath broken clouds,

the box elders heavy with dew.

Even the eldest box elders from which a true dream

can drop while the coldest rain that isn't quite snow

rises through your slicker,

the cardinals flickering over the fields and

carrying whatever's left of their only known reason why.

The horn signals a shift change in Shenzhen.

The neighbor's television mumbles the casualty report

through the wall, proving urgency

always overcomes distance.

So we carry on, measure our horses in hands,

whiskey in fingers, pools in feet,

while the dairy farm moves in upstream

and a few more green frogs vanish.

I can't get this out of my head because I can't get out of my head.

Any mantra is half about the insight,

half the bodily repetition.

Step, step, together. Left, right, left.

The trees rustle with plastic Walgreens bags

roosting during their circular parking lot migration patterns,

the remains of the older thing

always congratulating the new,

which is how confetti was invented.

Full disclosure here: the arrival of evening

isn't the dawn of nothing,

it's simply the most tangible evidence of absence,

the worst wind making no new shapes,

another life we'll live in our mind

that will never be fully believed.

Beneath a submarine of sky,

the cardinals will go on for a while,

as if we could live without the sun,

and it's here where we imagine

the first word might have been spoken

even as we know it was never heard.

So we diversify our futures

as the satellites deliver

a little more of our banal chatter,

the desperate calls from the frozen food aisle,

coats still on, so far from the waves that hit the distant beaches

and retreat, leaving a mile of used toothbrushes

to fade in the sun. Just cardinals,

intimate strangers, never still.

If heaven really does mean an eternity

being surrounded by those we love,

then maybe the great surprise that awaits us there

is the degree to which we'll miss

this thin sense of refuge most of all,

like being the only one in the cineplex

on a Wednesday afternoon,

feet slung over an empty seat back,

warm in the Dolby thunder.

The triumphant aliens wander

what's left of Wall Street

as you sit there just long enough

to read a few peculiar names

from the seemingly endless credits stream

out of some invisible bond

of courtesy and curiosity,

before you emerge back into the street light

to carve your own likeness out of thin air,

one you'll never recognize long enough

to call done.

Acknowledgments

Thank you to the editors of the following publications for first publishing many of the poems in this book: *Big Bell; Conduit; Forklift, Ohio; Green Mountains Review; Konundrum Engine Literary Review; The Laurel Review; MiPoesias; METRO; The Morning News; notnostrums;* and *Water-Stone Review.*

"40 Fortunes" was also published as a chapbook by Laminated Cats Press. Thank you Ben Kopel.

"Beware of False Friends" was also included on the compact disc *Salon Saloon: The Middle Years.* Thank you Andy Sturdevant and Works Progress.

"The Minneapolis Poem" was also included in the anthology *This Land.* Thank you This Land Press and Abby Wendle.

"The Painter" was interpreted as a short film by Motionpoems. Thank you Todd Boss.

"Pastor Pastoral" was also included in the *Green Mountains Review 25th Anniversary Issue.* Thank you Neil Shepherd and Jacob White.

"Silly String Theory" was also published as a broadside by the Center for the Book at the University of Iowa. Thank you Jill Kambs and Karen Carcia.

"Silly String Theory" was also included in *The New Census: An Anthology of Contemporary American Poetry.* Thank you Rescue Press, Kevin González, and Lauren Shapiro.

I'm grateful for the encouragement I've received from my family and friends, both near and far. And very special thanks to my poetry sister Amanda Nadelberg, and my editor Jeff Shotts, for their careful attention to earlier drafts of this book.

Dobby Gibson is the author of *Polar* (Alice James Books), which won the Beatrice Hawley Award, and *Skirmish* (Graywolf Press). He lives in Minneapolis.

It Becomes You is set in Arno Pro, a face designed by Robert Slimbach and named after the river that runs through Florence. This book was designed by Ann Sudmeier. Composition by BookMobile Design and Digital Publisher Services, Minneapolis, Minnesota. Manufactured by Versa Press on acid-free 30 percent postconsumer wastepaper.